Wanderings of an Ordinary Pilgrim

Tim Bete

Cover design based on a photo
of a sunset on the Camino de Santiago in Spain.

www.GrayRising.com

Copyright © 2019, Tim Bete
All rights reserved.

ISBN: 9781090712646

Available in print and e-book on Amazon.com.

This collection of poems is dedicated
to all pilgrims who search for God.
May you meet Him on the journey.

TABLE OF CONTENTS

Preface.. 6

Departures
After the Fall 10
Where is My Heart?.............................. 12
God is Everywhere.............................. 13
Death Again 14
The Creator 16
A Down-Stripping at 30...................... 17
The Word.. 18

Journeys
Wheels Down...................................... 20
The Overseer 21
Lost Things 22
Six Houses.. 24
Leaving Fatima 26
Abrading Grace 27
Good Friday in Salamanca 28
In Santerem 30
Avila 31
Mary's River 32
Relics.. 33
At the Baths.. 34
Consolation 35
Bus Trip to Pope Francis 36

Sojourns

The Church 38
Impassible 40
First Snow 41
Divine Office of the Shovel...........................42
A Lemon Sorbet of Words............................43

Returns

Return of the High School Retreat...............46
Orphaned..47
The Longest Road 48
Precipice of Love...50
The Roads Not Taken 51
At Six 52
Pilgrim's End...53
Over My Shoulder 54

Notes 58
Acknowledgments 62
About the Author...63
Other Books by Tim Bete 64

PREFACE

When I went on a pilgrimage with my family a few years ago, I decided not to take along a camera but rather a notebook. I jotted down thoughts, ideas and images that struck me while traveling through Portugal, Spain, France and Italy.

I wrote a handful of poems during the pilgrimage and after I returned, meditated upon the pages of the notebook until they became additional poems. Some of the poems are about places we visited, while others were simply inspired by Scripture and prayer during the journey.

The pilgrimage wasn't my first. I'd been to Portugal and Italy before and also to the Czech Republic, Croatia, Bosnia and Herzegovina, the United Kingdom, China and Australia, although not all of those trips were pilgrimages in the traditional sense.

Within the United States I've travelled to the Holy Hill Basilica in Wisconsin; the Basilica of the National Shrine of the Little Flower in San Antonio; Our Lady, Queen of the Most Holy Rosary Cathedral in Ohio; and, while a student at The Catholic University of America, lived for a year within sight of the Basilica of the National Shrine of the Immaculate Conception in Washington, DC.

It's funny how we will often travel a great distance to find God while not looking for Him as carefully while at home. As I reflected on my longer pilgrimages, many of my ordinary, routine pilgrimages came to mind—things such as my commute to work each day and the slow passing of seasons.

Like the disciples on the road to Emmaus, we meet God as much on the road as at our destination. Whether you are reading this book while on a pilgrimage to a foreign land or while sitting at home, I hope you find in it an experience of our most-loving God, who is even more excited about journeying to us than we are to Him.

May God bless you in all your travels.

— Tim Bete

P.S. When I read poetry, I often wonder what inspired the poet to use a certain metaphor or phrase. At the end of this book, I've included notes that provide a few thoughts on some of the poems.

DEPARTURES

"In those days he departed to the mountain to pray,
and he spent the night in prayer to God."

— Luke 6:12

After the Fall (or The Pilgrimage Begins)

Outside the garden,
they stood weeping:
bitter tears mingling

with the heat of the day;
bees flitting in hyacinth,
a sunbird in a mulberry tree.

The breeze that once
signaled the Lord walking
nearby, now highlighted

the distressing void—
scent of fruit still
hanging on their lips,

muddled minds grinding
the reality of the loss,
and the what next?

why us?
where to?
Then a familiar voice:

"look for me"—
not audible but
penetrating and deeper

than the cars.
"Search for me"—
a journey to last

until the end of their days.
A journey to last until
the end of my days.

Where is My Heart?

One foot on the dock,
the other on the gunwale;
weight shifting from land to sea;
water below ravenous
to swallow my indecision.

O God, who for love
of me made both
the gap and the brine,
may I leap to You,
without looking back.

God is Everywhere

and every when
and every why
and every how;

yet He stooped
to create me
in His image,
so I wouldn't be alone.

Death Again

Dying once was not
enough for Lazarus,

who was granted
a two-fold path—

a second life,
a second chance.

Not that the second
time would be a charm,

with chief priests
plotting to kill him

and the annoying
celebrity of it all.

But as he woke
from dusk's dull dream,

stiff muscles shrouded
along with face

and ears and eyes,
the smell of myrrh

mingled with a memory
of his own rotting flesh,

and he was no longer
afraid to die

as he had been the first,
when he passed alone—

longing only for his
Savior's voice,

that he now heard calling
from outside the tomb.

The Creator

Who scoffs at the potter
with a lump of clay on the wheel,
saying the lump is not a vase,
when the wheel hasn't turned?

Who chastises the sculptor
next to a marble block,
saying the block is not a figure,
when the hammer hasn't swung?

Who rebukes the blacksmith
with iron still in the fire,
saying the glowing shaft isn't a sword,
when the anvil hasn't rung?

When the potter
in midwork shapes,
and the sculptor half done
works his chisel deftly,
and the blacksmith heats
the sword a second time,

the beauty sleeps,
awaiting the awakening;
not to be judged
until the creator is finished.

A Down-Stripping at 30

The trappings of faith fit me so well:
religious books, Saint statues and crucifixes;
Rosary beads, Bible study groups and holy cards.

But when asked about my relationship with Jesus,
I squirmed like the dream one has of showing
up at school wearing only underwear.

I recall answering, "our relationship is great,"
while thinking, "I do not know the man";
at once standing with Peter in the courtyard.

I don't mind answers, it's the questions that vex me;
questions that nag you throughout the night
and into a lifetime of conversion.

The Word

I binged on a banquet
of noise, until all sound
was emetic to my ears,
each new cacophony
retched out like spoiled
food eaten in haste.

I read the Word
and the Word in my soul
called back—an echo
reverberating;
a heart beating;
and I knew the Word lived.

JOURNEYS

"What woman having ten coins and losing one would not light a lamp and sweep the house, searching carefully until she finds it?"

— Luke 15:8

Wheels Down

Have I arrived or returned?
It's difficult to tell, one airport

looking like all the others.
I often have the sense of traveling

without going anywhere,
as if the plane was just a box

to hide in while the outside
was rearranged. But no matter

where I go, I find God
has beaten me there.

The Overseer

God hangs on my kitchen wall,
overseeing dinner each evening;
meatloaf and mashed potatoes
on Tuesday; chicken on Sunday.

Hanging from the rearview mirror
of my car, He observes my drive
to work; monitoring traffic jams,
potholes, and fluctuating gas prices.

He hangs in my office, overseeing
the writing of letters and reports;
check signings; phone calls;
and the occasional meeting.

Such an amiable God,
who willingly watches the mundane
parts of my life—parts that sometimes
don't interest even me.

Lost Things

St. Anthony of Lisbon,
patron saint of lost things,
did not answer the prayer
to find my lost youth,

saying it wasn't lost
but rather squandered—
a cruel technicality
I did not wish to hear.

Nor did he help find
my lost patience,
saying I had never really
possessed any to begin with,

and what had not been lost,
could not be found.
When I asked him about
an embarrassing incident

in which I lost my dignity,
all he found for me was a dose
of humility, and a memory
I did not want to recount.

Sure, St. Anthony is great
when something small
has been misplaced,
but give him a difficult issue

and you'll find he is the patron
saint of brutal honesty,
making you wish
your car keys were missing.

Six Houses

I remember the swing in the basement;
a litter of kittens near the washer;
bunk beds and chicken pox;
a large red leather Bible.

I remember the widow's walk;
the ship's clock chiming each hour;
fenced yard and flower boxes;
figurehead Amanda adorning the wall.

I remember the gray slate sink;
the food pantry with field mice;
the rocking chair in the kitchen;
encyclopedias behind the dinner table.

I remember blossoming rose hip bushes;
the gurgling of the fish tank;
stone patio and outdoor shower;
car tires crunching the gravel drive.

I remember the tossed-stone berm;
steaks sizzling on the grill; sprawling
deck and chairs; early morning fog
and the smell of coffee.

I remember frenetic bird feeders;
breakfast dishes placed out
each evening; and rooms patiently
waiting each time we visit.

But most of all I remember you—
reading the red leather Bible
and reminding me to be safe up
on the widow's walk.

I remember you silhouetted
by blossoming rose hips
and nursing in the rocking chair
in the kitchen. I remember you

putting out the breakfast dishes
in the evening and tossing
a salad just before the steaks
were brought in from the grill.

Six houses in which God
was always present;
six houses in which you planted
the seeds of faith;
six houses with one love
that made each a home.

Leaving Fatima

The fog weaves
through the trees

as we drive into the hills;
oak and olive branches

piercing the haze.
The smoky blanket

covers our heads,
then allows us

to peek out.
Like candles burning

in the grotto,
sun slowly melts

away the mist.
Oh, Fatima,

the shining one,
how your children

taught us to pray
but now we must part,

taking with us
our Mother's heart.

Abrading Grace

My persistence in prayer
did not wear down God,
as did the widow with the judge,
but rather wore down me,
slowly weathering away my will,
like water coursing over rock—

at first an imperceptible groove,
then eroding into a great ravine,
until I could no longer remember
for what I'd been praying.
I suppose it had been important
at one time, but now my fatigue

causes me to rest in prayer,
too exhausted to bother God
with today's trivialities;
He does the heavy lifting
and I do the accepting,
which is what He'd planned all along.

Good Friday in Salamanca

The smells of strong coffee
and wet street mingle above
white wax dots that marble

the cobblestones.
Even at this early hour,
processions begin anew;

fresh candles in hand,
along with drums and trumpets
cleaving the morning air.

Through the narrow avenues,
18 sets of feet carry
each flowered float,

escorting our Lord and Lady;
the locals so comfortable
with the sights and sounds,

it is easy to imagine
that these processions
occur every day and not

only during Holy Week.
Their faith grips God
like their naked feet

on the cold stone and mortar—
alive with anticipation,
every irregularity felt,

as they adore His dead
body and await
His resurrection.

In Santerem

With long, careful strokes,
a man whitewashes a wall

outside St. Stephen's Church;
each new stripe turning

dingy stain to bright ivory.
Inside, a mother silently

prays, enjoying the coolness
of the stone tile while her

infant sleeps in a stroller;
a short rest before continuing

the errands of the day.
How is it that so great

a God watches
over ordinary lives,

revealing Himself
in the commonplace?

And with a God who gives
Himself as bread,

how can anything
be commonplace again?

Avila

Behind the cloister wall,
she cups fresh silence
in her wrinkled hands
and drinks. Absorbed

and uncertain if time
is measured in minutes
or eternities.
Like sunrise warming

the evening's darkness,
each wound and desire
is laid before Him,
without a single word.

Mary's River

The Gave de Pau slid past,
keeping vigil on Lourdes' shrine;
dappled trout sipping flies off its surface,
as I waited my turn for the baths.

Rivers have always been cathedrals
for me; standing waist-deep
in a gliding baptismal font,
the rhythm of fisherman and fly rod

mimicking priest and thurible;
clouds of gnats like incense billowing
over the water. What a God
it is, who would pick fishermen

as friends, knowing full well
that after He had risen, they would
count their 153 large fish
before paying attention to him.

Relics

Why did the thorns
have to pierce
their maker's head,

and the wood hold
its creator's hands
outstretched?

Did the iron cry
out when driven
through its master's

hands or the steel
wail as it punctured
the side of its king?

Each desired only
to do His bidding,
His blood bathing

them until they were
transformed from
common to holy—

relics that preached
His death and hoped
in His resurrection.

At the Baths

She stood in line silently:
matriarch-mother, child-bearer,
cancer-carrier, desperate-one.

Tears—oh, the tears of waiting.

She entered the bath silently:
blushing-bride, helpmate, companion,
malignant-growth, powerless-one.

Tears—oh, the tears of waiting.

She dried herself off silently:
baby-girl, daughter, blood-sister,
metastasis, dependent-one.

Tears—oh, the tears of waiting.

She rode to the airport silently:
sacrosanct, hallowed, hollowed,
prayerful, hopeful-one.

Tears—oh, the tears of waiting.

Consolation

God responded to my prayer
the instant He knew of it—
which wasn't an instant at all,
but rather a time before time.

He knew who I was before
I was, loving me into existence
until I sprung awake, yelling,
"where are you,"

for I could not perceive
His immensity—my entire life
a consolation,
that I was too close to see.

Bus Trip to Pope Francis

For a dozen hours I rode on a bus
with 32 high schoolers to see
Pope Francis, our decades of the Rosary
interspersed with Disney movies.

A strange thing, listening on my earbuds
to Benedictine nuns and Dominican sisters
chanting *Duo Seraphim* and *Christe Sanctorum*
while watching images from *Tangled*

and *High School Musical*—Gabriella and Troy
attempting to discover if they were meant
for each other. But perhaps no stranger
than watching teenagers embrace life

with an enthusiasm I envy and an outpouring
of love that reveals they grasp their faith
much better than I imagined. Some might
call them the future of the Church

but it seems to me they are the Church
of today as much as anyone—
accepting of God's grace and each other—
unsure what is ahead but willing to rely

on God's providence as they share their lunches
with the homeless—arms intertwined,
dancing through the streets of Philadelphia,
on a pilgrimage to see Pope Francis.

SOJOURNS

"Come to me, all you who labor
and are burdened,
and I will give you rest."

— Matthew 11:28

The Church

The narthex, the nave, the steeple,
the transept, the columns, the corbel,
the buttress, the portal, the plaster,
the gold, the marble, the silver.

The Stations of the Cross
carved in Paris and shipped
in the hold of a schooner
on its way to Boston.

The bondstone, the bed joints, the mortar,
the granite, the weep holes, the stretcher.

The Irish mason who ate
his lunch sitting on scaffolding,
legs dangling in the air
200 feet above the ground.

The bull's-eye, the rondel, the solder,
the leading, the fish tape, the badger.

The stained glass designed
in Germany by a man whose
apprentice was engaged
to his oldest daughter.

The bird's-mouth, the cheek-cut, the gable,
the stringer, the molding, the spandrel.

The carpenter who kept
a holy card of St. Stanisław
in his pocket, given to him
by his mother in Krakow.

The arches, the ambo, the pillars,
the chancel, the pew rows, the altar.

My heart and knees joined
to those who lived long ago,
whose hands forged
the sacramental frame

in which I kneel;
the mysteries of their craft
caressing the mysteries
of God.

Impassible

Your perfect passion,
beyond emotion and pain,
fills every crevice,
like water flowing
through rock fissures.

In each moment,
all mercy given,
all love loosed,
nothing held back;
only the great "I am."

Even when I sin,
I drown in Your
inescapable presence,
no crashing waves
but rather a burial

in Your silent depths.
You are an impassible
God—my sweet impassible
God, who knew my sin,
yet created me anyway.

First Snow

How I yearn for death to disguise itself again
in the yellow, red and orange colors of fall;

a veil hiding the mystery of being. Anticipating
the twilight behind each leaf, knowing

part of me must go with them.
My soul lingers in the chilly lull—

time standing still; a delicate balance
between breath and beyond; soaking

in the moment, tender sorrow turning to dusk—
until the first flakes begin to fall.

Divine Office of the Shovel

In the darkness
of the winter's
early morning,
there is a caesura

between the *skeriiiit*
of the shovel blade
and the *phlumph*
of snow upon

snowbank—
a pause filled
with only the sound
of my breath.

In those sacred
moments, before the sun
and snowplow,
my shovel echoes

through the street,
offering prayer intentions
for neighbors still
asleep in their beds.

A Lemon Sorbet of Words

You read this poem, wondering
if it will have a point or waste
your time, and now three lines in,

you're still uncertain. But perhaps
"waste" is too strong a word,
for even lemon sorbet—

served between courses
of a meal—has its purpose.
The way an hour of boredom

waiting alone in an airport
can cleanse the palate of your mind—
an hour you would not choose

to spend, but in hindsight
thank God for because
of His quiet presence.

44

RETURNS

"The servant said to him, 'Your brother has returned
and your father has slaughtered the fattened calf
because he has him back safe and sound.'"

— Luke 15:27

Return of the High School Retreat

They entered the chapel like dogs
coming in from the cold,
skittering across the kitchen floor

in an attempt to make contact
with every person in the room—
scratches behind ears,

wet noses pressed against hands,
with a brief slobber-stop at the water dish.
And for a moment, the altar transformed

into a kitchen table, the Father
quietly sitting, taking it all in,
as fathers often do,

the occassion for reverence
a distant thought, as He smiled,
simply glad they were home again.

Orphaned

Abandoned by a once intimate God,
I lay naked on the canyon floor,
bare skin exposed to the elements
and circling birds of prey.

Iced by night and scorched by day,
for weeks and months, I lay still,
but could not die or even sleep;
I longed to close my eyes.

Then just as quickly as He had gone,
God was the canyon and the sky;
His largeness was his largess,
and I knew that He remained.

The Longest Road

How many days did he walk,
mulling over words he would say
to a father scorned and insulted?
Replaying scenarios in his mind.

Still so focused on himself
all he could think of was,
"I will say this and he
will probably say that."

Reliving each burning memory.
Scourging himself for past deeds.
Recreating pain and misery.
Kindling the blaze of a private Hell.

And if for a moment he considered
forgiveness, he quickly threw fuel
on his pain until it exploded
with all thought of mercy consumed.

At home, a father's love burned.
Thinking only of his son's return,
not a second spent on past deeds—
the fire of hope sustained him.

A father filled with the
cremating blaze of compassion,
turning all memories of sin
forever into ash.

When they met on the road:
an embrace, a kiss, an apology unheard—
their two fires collided,
one of pain, the other of love,

and at that moment
the son could not remember
why he had left; nor could he fathom
the thought of ever leaving again.

Precipice of Love

Standing at the precipice of Love,
my toes tightly grip the edge,
longing to be on firmer ground,
far from the depths
where Mercy's fire consumes.

But my soul commands my feet to stay,
powered by desire's stark yearning;
with a languished gaze into the abyss,
I wait; I wait; I wait
to hear Love's soft call.

The pull, the plunge, the fall, oh Love!

Yet gone so quickly.

I ache for the day when my soul
says, "I go alone this time,"
despite my body's desperate cries—
diving, diving; plummeting
into Love forever.

The Roads Not Taken

Perhaps Robert Frost
was right about diverging
roads and woods;
thousands of forked

decisions in a life—
I couldn't go down
them all if I lived
five hundred years.

Each opportunity
offers a choice between
regret and remorse;
the loss of one option

or the suffering to accept
the will's momentary desire.
Yet in each choice,
God's grace leads—

or follows—
turning poor decisions
to profit; allowing me
to find my way home.

At Six

I chanted epic poems to You,
while on the swing, legs
keeping time to the rhythmic
groan of stressed metal bars.

And now 50 years later,
those poems echo in my ears—
not the words but the cadence—
like hearing someone speak

in tongues or a song somewhere
in the distance. Who are you
that you would dry up
all my longings except for You?

Like a dying man who takes
one bite and is satisfied, unable
to take another, past pleasures
barren, stripped of any semblance

of joy. Yet I desperately long
to eat more, a hunger greater
than any I have known—to chant
epic poems with You forever.

Pilgrim's End

I searched to find a God
who was not lost,
and did not need to be found—
He was already here.

Over My Shoulder

Every ten years
or so, I reflect back
on my decade-old bewilderment
and how inadequate

was my concept of God;
and my prayer life;
and my faith—for starters.
Today once again,

I go through the exercise,
writing weak words;
knowing in the future
I will scoff at today's understanding;

today's idea;
today's vision.
The more I know God,
the more unknowable

He becomes
and the more foolhardy
His love for me appears.
But perhaps that's His point—

that knowing can only live
within the mystery;
certainty a clouded
reflection at best.

I travelled to distant lands
to find Him and returned
with religious trinkets
and a backpack full of questions—

more than when I left—
providing fodder for prayer
and a reason to begin thinking
about my next pilgrimage.

NOTES

A few thoughts about some of the poems in this collection...

Where is My Heart?: A gunwale is the top edge of a boat. For a smaller boat, it is where you place your foot as you board. If you're not careful, you can end up with one foot on the dock and the other on the gunwale, with the water beneath you. (I know this from personal experience.) The word gunwale comes from a Middle English word describing the part of the boat used to support the guns or cannons.

Death Again: Sometimes I'll read a Scripture passage and notice something for the first time. That happened to me one morning, when I read John 12: 10-11: "And the chief priests plotted to kill Lazarus too, because many of the Jews were turning away and believing in Jesus because of him."

A Down-Stripping at 30: When I was 30, I had a spiritual director who always asked the question, "So how are you and Jesus?" The question made me squirm and I suspect he knew it because he never failed to ask the question. Obviously, he was a good spiritual director.

The Word: *Emetic* means vomit-inducing. Those of the types of words you learn when your mother is a nurse.

The Overseer: Some days you just notice all the crucifixes in your life.

Lost Things: St. Anthony of Padua, also known as St. Anthony of Lisbon (Portugal) where he was born, is the Patron Saint of lost articles. He has this title because a novice who left his community took with him St. Anthony's Psalter (Book of Psalms).

Anthony prayed for the return of the book and eventually the novice rejoined the Franciscan Order, bringing with him Anthony's book. That Psalter is now at the Franciscan Friary in Bologna, Italy.

Six Houses: I wrote this poem as a present for my mother on her 80th birthday. The poem describes the six houses in which I lived with her and the rest of my family, mostly as a child. Three of the houses were in the same town in western Massachusetts; two were located on Cape Cod; and one in Maine.

A widow's walk is a platform on the roof of a house that provides a good view of the ocean. They were common in New England houses located near the water. The name *widow's walk* comes from a wife looking to see if her husband's ship had returned.

A figurehead is a carved wooden decoration found on the bow of a ship. We had one on the wall of our kitchen in Cape Cod. It was of a woman's upper body—Amanda Fenwick to be specific.

Abrading Grace: Luke 18: 1-8 is the parable of the persistent widow. The widow fervently prays that the judge will give her justice. Perhaps the greatest thing she received was she learned to pray without ceasing. There is a reason God puts judges in our lives.

Good Friday in Salamanca: During Holy Week In Salamanca, Spain, a procession of floats with realistic wooden sculptures streams through the streets. Penitents follow the floats, carrying candles, flags and crosses. Many of the processions include bands with drums and trumpets. Each float is carried by a team of *brothers of the paso*. *Paso* means float. The floats are very heavy, taking at least a dozen people to carry them. The brothers of the paso do not wear shoes during the procession.

In Santerem: In 1247, A Eucharistic miracle occurred in Santerem, Portugal, in which a host turned to actual flesh and blood. The miraculous Host is on display in the Church of St. Stephen, which was renamed the Church of the Holy Miracle. It is one of Portugal's most-visited pilgrimage sites.

Avila: Avila, Spain, is where St. Teresa of Jesus began her reform of the Carmelite Order.

Mary's River: John 21:11 reads, "So Simon Peter went over and dragged the net ashore full of one hundred fifty-three large fish." I've often found it curious that in seeing the Lord after His resurrection, Peter still counted his catch. That sounds like something I would do.

The Church: This poem lists different elements of masonry, carpentry, stained glass and other architectural features that make up a church. The number of gifts needed to create the great beauty of a single church is simply astounding to me.

Impassible: The Catholic Church's teaching of the impassibility of God is a difficult concept to understand. In a nutshell, it means that because God is unchanging, He does not feel suffering, joy or pain, in the way we understand those things. He is only love.

Divine Office of the Shovel: A *caesura* is a silent pause between sounds.

Orphaned: *Largeness* describes size. *Largess* is generosity in giving.

The Roads Not Taken: The poem, *The Road Not Taken*, was written by Robert Frost in 1916. It just entered the public domain, so I will share it with you here.

The Road Not Taken
Two roads diverged in a yellow wood,
And sorry I could not travel both
And be one traveler, long I stood
And looked down one as far as I could
To where it bent in the undergrowth;

Then took the other, as just as fair,
And having perhaps the better claim,
Because it was grassy and wanted wear;
Though as for that the passing there
Had worn them really about the same,

And both that morning equally lay
In leaves no step had trodden black.
Oh, I kept the first for another day!
Yet knowing how way leads on to way,
I doubted if I should ever come back.

I shall be telling this with a sigh
Somewhere ages and ages hence:
Two roads diverged in a wood, and I—
I took the one less traveled by,
And that has made all the difference.

At Six: One of my favorite things when I was a child was to spend time on a swing set. The more stress put on our swing set by the motion of going back and forth, the more the metal bars made groaning sounds.

Acknowledgements

The Longest Road and *Bus Trip to Pope Francis* were originally published in the book, *The Raw Stillness of Heaven.*

Lost Things was originally published in *Presence: A Journal of Catholic Poetry 2019.*

Scripture texts in this work are taken from the New American Bible, revised edition © 2010, 1991, 1986, 1970 Confraternity of Christian Doctrine, Washington, D.C. and are used by permission of the copyright owner. All Rights Reserved. No part of the New American Bible may be reproduced in any form without permission in writing from the copyright owner.

ABOUT THE AUTHOR

Tim Bete is a member of the Secular Order of Discalced Carmelites and often trades poems with his oldest daughter, who is a Dominican Sister. (He says she is the best writer in the family.)

While Tim has been a writer for much of his life, he only started writing poetry after he entered his fifties and began spending a significant amount of time in silent prayer. The more time he spent in silence, the greater the ease he had writing poetry. In a way, Tim's poems are his prayer journal.

Tim is the author of *In the Beginning…There Were No Diapers*, a humorous book of essays on the mysteries of parenting (Ave Maria Press). His writing has appeared in several editions of the Amazing Grace anthology series (Ascension Press) as well as the *Christian Science Monitor*, the Poet and Contemplative Blog of the Discalced Carmelite Friars (Province of St. Therese) and *Presence: A Journal of Catholic Poetry*. This is his second book of poetry. His first is *The Raw Stillness of Heaven*.

Tim is also poetry editor for the Catholic Poetry Room on the Integrated Catholic Life website— www.IntegratedCatholicLife.org.

You can contact him at www.GrayRising.com.

ALSO BY TIM BETE

The Raw Stillness of Heaven

Through poems about prayer, conversion and faith, Tim Bete shares his search for God—a search that is common to each of us. Somewhere in the intersection of holy silence and the struggles of daily life, God appears: in a winter evening walk, in the smell of incense at church, in a blue patio chair, in the Sacrament of Confession. More than a collection of poems, this book is a prayer journal—a glimpse into the faith journey of the poet.

Reviews

"Beautiful and very accomplished."
— Sally Read, poet and author of *Night's Bright Darkness*

"Gorgeous Catholic poetry."
— Leslie Lynch

"If you are Catholic and think that you do not like poetry, this book will change your mind."
— W.R. Rodriguez, author of *The Bronx Trilogy*

"You have touched my heart, mind and soul with your unique prayerful poems in a way I can't describe."
— Sheila Buska, author of *Paul's World*

Available in Kindle and paperback at Amazon.com.

Printed in Great Britain
by Amazon